# FIREMEN OF INDUSTRY

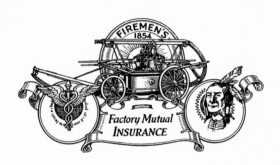

# Firemen of Industry

*by*

*Frederick T. Moses*

*1854-1954*

*The Hundredth Anniversary of*
FIREMEN'S MUTUAL INSURANCE COMPANY

150 South Main Street
Providence, Rhode Island

Copyright 1954 by Firemen's Mutual Insurance Company

# Contents

# Foreword

MAY 6, 1954 marks the One Hundredth Anniversary of the Firemen's Mutual Insurance Company.

The history of the Company has coincided with and is a pivotal part of the story of the companies with which it is associated, that group commonly known as the Associated Factory Mutuals.

Throughout its existence the Firemen's has found its customers, not among industries in the community of its home office, but principally in those industrial areas of the United States and Canada that have been so highly developed during the last fifty years.

We do not propose to detail the much-told history of fire insurance itself and we shall only briefly touch on that part of the background of the Factory Mutuals which needs clarification. Our story is rather that of the contribution of the Firemen's Mutual Insurance Company to the success of Factory Mutual insurance and to the solution of one of the most pressing problems of our national economy—the prevention of loss by fire.

FREDERICK T. MOSES
*Chairman of the Board*

Firemen's Mutual Insurance Co.
Providence, R. I.

*Early symbol of the Firemen's.*

# 1

# The Pioneer Days

IT IS SAID that in 1735 an unsuccessful effort was made to establish a fire insurance company in America. There was little demand for insurance; most of the country was still in the pioneer stage, its principal occupation agriculture. There were only a few substantial centers of population along the Atlantic Coast. Since manufacturing was forbidden during the Colonial period by the British Acts of Trade, the fire insurance problem was confined almost entirely to dwellings, stores and warehouses.

The beginning of fire prevention and insurance centered around Philadelphia and the activities of Benjamin Franklin. As early as 1696 the Provincial Government passed certain legislation concerning the cleaning of chimneys. Later, with the growth of population, fires increased and private fire-fighting companies were formed, patterned after earlier organizations of this character that had been established in England. Philadelphia's first was organized by Franklin in 1736, and in the next fifty years it was followed by many others.

Fires were constantly destroying property and in most cases people were financially unable to rebuild. It was usual to take up public subscriptions and to give benefits in theatres in an effort to rehabilitate them. Then, in 1752, Franklin organized the first fire insurance company in America. It was a mutual and known as The Philadelphia Contributionship For The Insurance Of Houses From Loss By Fire; it is still outstanding in the insurance world after an experience covering over two hundred years.

Two principles were then established that were to constitute the fundamentals of mutual insurance for two centuries thereafter. One was the careful selection of risks and the second was to inspect them.

The Contributionship would not insure a risk until it had been inspected and had complied with any necessary recommendations for improvement. The inspection work was first carried on by two directors of the company, building contractors by trade, whose experience qualified them to understand hazardous construction and provide for improvement. The fire hazards of the day were obvious and not too difficult to eliminate,

*Volunteers of Engine Company 21 and Hose Company 60 race through New York. The date is 1854.*

with the result that fire losses on individual properties were considerably reduced.

There still remained the hazard of a general conflagration, which increased with the growth in population, and the Contributionship passed through some difficult experiences until it realized the necessity for building up a reserve to stabilize the company and carry it through an occurrence resulting from causes over which it had no control. Thereafter the company was highly successful.

In the period from 1790 to 1800 marine insurance, which then constituted the bulk of the business, was divided among individual underwriters. When the War of 1812 forced a general cessation of business among marine companies, attention turned to fire insurance and countless companies were organized in different sections of New England. The general aim of these groups was financial speculation, rather than an attempt to provide simple indemnity from disaster. During the same period there was a superabundance of capital in London and this led to the formation there of all manner of companies insuring all sorts of contingencies. They would cover the performance of bargains, titles, commercial credits, robbery, judgment of debts, and payment of dividends on securities. They would indemnify travelers against loss of life or property by highwaymen, against captivity by pirates, against lying, or against death by drinking Geneva (the old name for gin). Insurance reached into such novel fields as protection against divorce, and loss of female chastity. (Your historian is unable to ascertain what constituted proof-of-loss.)

After the Revolution, with the resulting relief from the onerous British restrictions on American manufacturing, the new nation slowly embarked upon its industrial development. Even then, as today, unusual industrial progress frequently resulted from the restraints imposed by war. The events preceding the War of 1812 caused the enactment of the Embargo Act, prohibiting much of the existing import and export business with the British. This changed the entire picture along the Atlantic Seaboard, particularly in New England, whose industry had been largely maritime. Ships lay idle in the harbors and enterprising Yankees turned to manufac-

*Fire leaves an early Massachusetts paper mill in ruins.*

turing the cotton and woolen goods no longer available from the mills of Lancashire. In 1816 Congress imposed a 25% duty on imported textiles, which further stimulated the business of the new mills. By 1835, the birth date of Factory Mutual insurance, New England had become the home of a booming textile industry, a circumstance which was to exist for many years.

In 1822 one Zachariah Allen built a textile mill in Rhode Island. The mill was of unusually substantial construction. An effort was made to isolate special hazards and provision was made to equip it with such crude fire-fighting apparatus as was then available. There were mutual insurance companies in existence at that time, but they did not insure factories. It was Allen's idea that their experience and methods could well be adapted to the growing textile industry. He therefore organized, in 1835, the Manufacturers Mutual Fire Insurance Company, the first of the Factory Mutual group.

Insurance was written on properties belonging mostly to friends and acquaintances. An elementary system of inspection was established; it resulted in a substantial reduction in the cost of insurance. The thinking of the age was not in terms of large individual units, so that, as time went on, rather than increase the size of the Manufacturers Mutual, numerous other companies were formed in order to provide the expanding textile industry with additional insurance capacity.

In the fifty years following Allen's initial venture the textile industry in New England experienced a period of phenomenal growth. The larger mills were located in Massachusetts and, profiting by Allen's experience, numerous insurance companies were organized in that state. One of these, the Boston Manufacturers, made great progress; in 1878 it elected as president a Bostonian, Edward Atkinson, who was to have a profound effect on the development of the Factory Mutual idea. Atkinson's experience, as treasurer of numerous mills, had been entirely in the field of finance. He was a man who combined the accountant's passion for statistics with the promoter's flair for publicity. He surrounded himself with many men of creative ability, correlated and accepted the credit for their accomplishments, which resulted in a series of uniform standards for construction and fire protection. The rather loosely knit but interdependent group of Factory Mutual Companies adopted these standards and implemented them through a joint Inspection Department which Atkinson had been able to set up.

In 1874 a Connecticut piano manufacturer named Parmalee invented and patented the automatic sprinkler. Many varieties of these devices were manufactured and their success in extinguishing fire led eventually to their adoption by the Factory Mutuals as an absolute requirement for all insured properties. The automatic sprinkler industry today owes the background of its success almost entirely to the Factory Mutuals. In the early days of the sprinkler manufacturer these devices were given no particular support by the stock fire insurance companies. Indeed, their use was actively opposed by the majority of insurance agents who did not relish the lower rate and a corresponding reduction in commission that

*Engine foreman shouts his orders through a speaking trumpet.*

the installation of such protective equipment eventually brought about.

In 1886 Atkinson hired a young engineer, John R. Freeman, and in a few years made him the head of the Inspection Department. Freeman brought into the Department a number of college-trained engineers from whom in future years were drawn the executive staffs of the different Factory Mutual Companies. Freeman was a prodigious worker; although his principal interest was his private practice as one of the country's foremost hydraulic engineers, yet he found time to develop the principles of fire protection on a sound engineering basis. To Freeman, more than anyone else, the country owes the establishment of the engineering fundamentals of the insurance business. In 1896 he went to Providence to assume the presidency of the Manufacturers Mutual.

The economic development of this nation divides itself roughly into three fifty-year periods. Following the Revolution there was a period of

*Engines like this were built to protect the textile mills.*

domestic turmoil. The Constitution was not ratified until 1788 and Washington did not retire from what could be considered an organized and operating government until 1797. The industry of the country was still almost entirely agricultural. Thus the first of these great fifty-year periods really begins about 1800, and the time from then until 1850 was devoted largely to the settlement of the country. Transportation by water received a tremendous boost from the invention of the steamboat in 1807. The Erie Canal, completed in 1825, opened a trail from the Atlantic to the Great Lakes and was an important factor in the settlement of the Western wilderness. In the 1840's and 1850's railroads began to lace the settled parts of the country into an interdependent whole. The first protective tariff was enacted in 1816, in itself a prime stimulant to domestic manufacturing.

The second period, from 1850 to 1900, particularly the latter part of this era, was one of enormous industrial progress. The textile industry was still the mainstay of New England and furnished the basis for most of the growth of that region. The Factory Mutual Companies had demonstrated the fundamental soundness of their original idea and had progressed along with this industry.

The managements of these mutual companies had reached a state of complete complacency. Their business was bounded geographically by the Alleghenies and the Potomac and consisted principally of textile mills, machine shops, and a few paper mills. Factory Mutual insurance was posed as an exclusive club in which membership was obtainable by suitable financial and social connections, supplemented by a willingness to maintain such fire protection standards as had been established.

Insurance costs were 75% less than those prevailing in the general insurance world and there was no important competition; in fact, the Factory Insurance Association, which is presently our only noticeable competitor, had just been organized.

Other industries, having observed the success of the Factory Mutuals in the textile field, sought the same protection for themselves. As a result, during the period 1870 to 1890, many new companies organized. Atkinson then proceeded to name his group the "Senior" companies and dubbed the new ones "Junior" companies in an effort to create in the public mind a sort of Dives and Lazarus relation, or perhaps to set up a defense for the lack of progress in new fields. At any rate, the names stuck until 1922 when all the Factory Mutuals consolidated into one group.

Those who organized the "Junior" companies had a realistic conception of what they wished to accomplish and it was definitely not the creation of an ivory tower. There were many sections of the country without the benefits of Factory Mutual insurance and many classes of industry that the "Senior" companies considered unqualified. Eventually most of the "Junior" companies were merged for economy into larger organizations. But the names of a few have historical interest.

The What Cheer Mutual was founded in Providence in 1873. President Lewis T. Downes was an aggressive and competent salesman. He secured the first Factory Mutual account in Canada, the Paton Manufacturing Company, a part of Dominion Textiles. His activities were largely responsible for opening the Canadian field to future development.

Philadelphia in 1880 contained a large number of moderate-sized textile factories. This was a natural development since many sources of water power existed in the surrounding country and much of the area was settled by textile workers from England. Under the influence of one of the vice presidents of the Pennsylvania Railroad and the Baldwin Locomotive Works, the Philadelphia Manufacturers Mutual Fire Insurance Company was organized in 1880. It was responsible for the development of the Factory Mutual idea in that section.

In 1887 Mr. Charles Deering, President of the Deering Company, which was later to be the nucleus for the International Harvester Company, organized the Protection Mutual Fire Insurance Company in Chicago. The progress subsequently made by the Factory Mutuals within two

*Washington Engine Company No. 1. was the pride of Brooklyn.*

*This ingenious contraption combined a ladder for the hosemen
with a bucket for rescue.*

hundred miles of Chicago resulted from the activities of this company.

The Baltimore Mutual was established in 1886 by numerous fertilizer manufacturers. The loss experience with this industry was unsatisfactory, however, and the Baltimore entered the Southern textile field. Its board of directors came to consist principally of Southern cotton manufacturers. Together with a New England company, the Mercantile, it was responsible for the entry and development of Factory Mutual insurance in the South.

The Cotton and Woolen Manufacturers Mutual Insurance Company was organized in 1875 by textile manufacturers to supply the need for a more aggressive company in Boston. It was soon followed by the Rubber to furnish mutual insurance to the rubber industry; and by the Industrial, a company organized by the Stone and Webster interests to insure electric light and power properties. These three companies were under the management of Benjamin F. Taft, a brother-in-law of William B. Whiting, who was chiefly responsible for the early success of the original Factory Mutual Inspection Department. A few years later Taft employed his son-in-law, Frederick W. Moses, as his assistant. Neither Taft nor Moses subscribed to the "exclusive club" theory. They believed that nearly every class of manufacturing could be protected in accordance with the Factory Mutual standards and develop the same low insurance costs that had been established in the textile field. From the beginning Taft was the leader of the "Junior" group.

Frederick W. Moses was born in Lebanon, New Hampshire, September 1, 1858. He was a direct descendant of Sergeant John Moses, an Englishman who received a grant of land from the King in 1639, in Portsmouth, New Hampshire, and was one of the early settlers of that community. Frederick W. Moses received his education in the public schools and at Tilton Academy, Tilton, New Hampshire. For the first five years of his business life he was associated with his father in the manufacture of furniture in Lebanon, New Hampshire, and New York City.

His outstanding personality resulted in his becoming the first real "salesman" of Factory Mutual insurance.

Early in his career Moses realized that the probable future industrial growth of the country was so great that an equal growth of the Factory Mutual system would be necessary if it hoped to provide the insurance capacity that industry would eventually require. As a result of his success with this idea in the Cotton and Woolen, Moses was elected President of the Firemen's in 1909, in which position his aggressive and farsighted attitude was to afford him much greater opportunities. Although the Firemen's had been in business since 1854, its management had been content to drift along with the tide and simply furnish additional mutual insurance capacity, the demand for which exceeded the supply. Within the limited circles in which the Factory Mutual Companies of that period had been content to operate, the Firemen's had only a very few small local accounts. Moses not only brought to the company the accomplishments of his pioneer work but established a starting point for the future creation of a strong organization. The many classes of risks he proved could be made eligible for insurance extended far beyond the initial concept of the founders of the original companies. It was his example that altered their limited, provincial outlook and made the Factory Mutual system nationally known.

There is probably no period in American history so important in the establishment of our present-day industrial civilization as the early part of the 20th century. Industrial accomplishment was then in its adolescence. The carryover of ideas from the previous century was typified by an editorial of that period in a prominent New York newspaper commenting that a man named Thomas A. Edison of East Orange, New Jersey, was possessed of the "crazy notion that he can supplant gas lights with an electric doodad." Or the famous story of Samuel F. B. Morse who offered his telegraph instrument as a gift to the people of the United States; Congress rejected it on the ground that it had "no practical value." In the period of which we are writing, new ideas such as those we now take in our stride were established only by overcoming much prejudice and complacency.

The background of a few of our nationally known industries cannot help but be of intense interest to all Americans; what we have accomplished for these few applies to the many; it is indeed the history of our business.

FREDERICK WILLIAM MOSES
*President of the Firemen's, 1909-1926.*

## THE GREAT WAGON-MAKER

IT WAS IN 1836 that John Studebaker built for himself three covered wagons, left his Dutch parents in Pennsylvania and started with his family and possessions for the West. His sons and, eventually, John himself landed in South Bend, Indiana, where they started their first wagon building enterprise with $68 and two sets of blacksmith tools.

The first years were precarious ones but by 1868 their business was on a sound basis and by 1876 they had the largest wagon and carriage works in the world. From ice wagons to elegant surreys, Studebaker presented the whole panorama of horse-drawn vehicles used in this country for decades.

Studebaker's entry into the automobile field began with the electric vehicle in 1900. Within a few years, however, this was abandoned in favor of the gasoline automobile, which finally was produced in 1908.

By 1920 the great transition was complete and the wagon business sold. Studebaker turned out to be the only one of the 5000 wagon manufacturers in the United States to make the change successfully into the automobile field.

In all the furore that has surrounded the automobile industry, it is perhaps not generally known that Studebaker is the oldest name in highway transportation in the world.

When Frederick W. Moses first insured Studebaker in the Factory Mutuals in 1896 the company's earlier insurance experience had not been a happy one. A series of fires had occurred in 1872, and in 1874 two-thirds of the plant had been left in ruins. The manufacture of wagons consisted principally of wood working, involving large lumber yards and many other special fire hazards. Existing insurance facilities did not possess the specialized knowledge necessary to advise the wagon-makers how to protect their property. Indiana was beyond the frontier to most of the "Senior" companies.

For 58 years, under our guidance, Studebaker has not had a crippling fire; after 58 years it is still insured with us.

## *THE AGRICULTURAL REVOLUTION*

W HILE AGRICULTURE is the oldest business in the world, its mechanical birth date may be said to be that of the perfection of the reaper by Cyrus Hall McCormick in 1831. In 1902 his eldest son, Cyrus H. McCormick, associated with Charles Deering of the Deering Harvester Company, organized International Harvester as a combination of five harvesting machinery manufacturers. Deering has already been mentioned in this account as one of the founders of the Protection Mutual Fire Insurance Company.

Underwriters rightly considered the manufacture of harvesting machinery a hazardous business. It required great amounts of dried and seasoned lumber, something which is still not regarded in insurance circles as too good a fire risk. In addition to lumber storage, there were large foundries, painting and dipping, twine mills and other collateral operations.

With Deering's interest in fire protection it was natural that he and his associates should turn to us for a solution of their problems; therefore it was quite soon after their organization that Moses placed their insurance in the Factory Mutuals.

Long study and thought were given to the successful solution of the fire protection problem. The management of Harvester was not only unusually capable but highly cooperative and, after over half a century of our connection with them, continues to be so. It is owing to them and to us of the Firemen's organization that no important interruption of their production because of fire has occurred during this long period.

Since the days of the first McCormick, America has changed from a predominantly agricultural nation into the world's greatest industrial power. If you would catalogue the great service which Harvester has rendered America in agricultural mechanization, think back to the original horse-drawn reaper and marvel over some of the products of today—crawler tractors, cotton pickers, corn pickers, hay balers, motor trucks, refrigeration devices—what next?

## NAPOLEON'S CANS FOR GRANDMOTHER'S KITCHEN

CANNING WAS INVENTED in the time of Napoleon to help feed his armies; the containers were of glass. Two years later the English invented the tin can and produced preserved foods for the British Navy. In this country can making was a slow, primitive process, carried on in small local shops, with the soldering done by hand; sixty cans per day was high production for one man.

Grandmother did her own canning or else did without. She entertained a deep suspicion, frequently well-founded, of the character of the commercial product; indeed, some grandmas had a vague feeling that the metal might be poisonous.

At the turn of the century the production of fruit and vegetables, meat and fish had far outgrown the capacity of the canning industry, yet food producers saw a year-round market for all these products if they could only be delivered to the public in good condition at all times.

In 1901 the American Can Company was formed as a national network of 123 local factories. Machinery had been developed but it was slow and cumbersome and, at best, could only make sixty cans per minute. The manufacture of the can was only part of the problem, since closing machinery had to be developed in order to use the can efficiently and economically. The next step was to put the can and its closing machinery nearer the source of the produce that was to be packed and distributed.

The accomplishments of this corporation over a period of years are truly remarkable. The machinery which once produced sixty cans a minute now has a capacity of over 450 cans; closing machines have been sold or leased to processors from coast to coast.

We who take for granted our cans of paint, of oil, of vacuum-packed coffee, even of beer, cannot realize the amount of research and ability that the production of these now commonplace products has required.

The newly formed American Can Company had as its treasurer and later its president, F. S. Wheeler. A farsighted executive, Wheeler realized that a loss by fire in a regional canning plant could cause the ruin of a seasonal crop through no fault of the producer.

Calling in Moses, he placed his insurance with the Factory Mutuals; it has been there ever since. No producer has lost his crop because of a disastrous fire!

## FASHIONS IN SMOKING

In THE MIDDLE of the 16th century tobacco was hailed as a cure-all for every ill that afflicted the human race; nicotine therapy soon was sweeping a disease-ridden world. Its social use followed some time later; its smoking was made fashionable by Sir Walter Raleigh in Queen Elizabeth's Court. In the early days of our Virginia Colony tobacco served as currency and sometimes established a credit base for the planters in England.

The early production of the manufactured product consisted of smoking tobacco, chewing tobacco and snuff, and the industry centered around Lynchburg, Virginia. Virginia at first had a near monopoly in the raising of tobacco, although this was eventually broken and it became one of the principal crops of North and South Carolina and, later, other states.

The manufacture of cigarettes in this country started in 1881. They were made by hand. The original cigarette machine was invented by James Bonsake in 1884. Inefficient as it was, it substantially reduced the cost of manufacture.

In 1890 James B. Duke organized the American Tobacco Company. It was reorganized in 1904 and retained almost complete control of all branches of the industry until split up by the Supreme Court in 1911.

The cigarette, which was to become the principal product of the industry, was still a very minor item; by some its use was considered to be sissy and by others a secret vice.

The risks of the tobacco industry were no more highly regarded by insurance companies than were its cigarettes by the public. Consequently insurance rates were high and there was no competition.

Moses induced the industry to protect its properties and finally persuaded the "Senior" Companies that cigarette plants could be made better fire risks than the beloved textile mills. Practically all of the component members comprising the original American Tobacco Company are still insured in the Factory Mutuals.

## *THE MAGIC FURNACE*

S<small>OME TIME ABOUT</small> 1890 a Canadian inventor named Willison was instrumental in the establishment of a little plant at Spray, North Carolina, and installed one of the new electric furnaces with which he was trying to manufacture aluminum. In 1892, after many futile attempts, a grayish substance came out. When Willison tried to quench it with water it gave off a burnable gas. The gray stuff was calcium carbide, the gas acetylene. This was the first commercial source of acetylene, which had been mainly a laboratory curiosity; no one had any conception of its useful possibilities. In 1898 Willison's discovery led to the formation of the original Union Carbide Company whose experiments resulted in practical carbide production methods, together with lamps and acetylene generators.

American towns too small for coal gas plants began to gleam with acetylene lamps, which continued in operation until superseded by electric lighting. Meanwhile, in France, oxyacetylene welding had been developed and in 1910 Carbide brought it into this country, where its use increased rapidly. What followed is a true saga of American enterprise and ability.

Needing oxygen to develop its oxyacetylene business completely, Carbide acquired control of Linde Air Products. The Prest-O-Lite Company, which produced a badly needed safe packing method for acetylene, was Carbide's largest customer and became a necessary addition to the group.

Carbide had too much calcium carbide furnace capacity in relation to what it could sell and, because it had contracted for continuous electric power and needed to take up the slack, it bought a plant in Niagara Falls and set up the Electro Metallurgical Company. Since little was known about the action of oxyacetylene flame on various metals, this company went to work to develop special welding rods. Later it was to engage in the production of various metal alloys, a venture which was to be extended through the acquisition of the Haynes Stellite Company.

From the beginning, the carbon electrodes required in the electric furnace operations of both Union Carbide Company and Electro Metallurgical Company were supplied largely by National Carbon Company, Inc. This company had been organized in 1886 for the manufacture of miscellaneous carbon products, the most important of which were carbons for electric arc street lights, then in universal use.

In 1917 all of these different corporations were combined into what is now Union Carbide and Carbon Corporation.

In the 1920's Carbide headed out on another tack. Research had brought forth the chemical possibilities of acetylene as a basic hydrocarbon for the foundation and synthesis of many commercial materials. The experience with acetylene led to the much more prolific hydrocarbon supply available in natural gas and petroleum products.

The new division, known as Carbide and Carbon Chemicals Corporation, had at hand a whole collection of experts from Prest-O-Lite and Linde, all experienced in the handling of gases. From this effort were to develop dozens of useful organic products; probably one of those more commonly known to the layman is ethylene glycol—the Prestone of our automobiles.

In a brief account it is almost impossible to put together a complete story of this corporation and its amazing accomplishments. The line of scientific advance, starting from Willison's little electric furnace and National Carbon's electrodes, leads to the world-wide use of oxyacetylene welding, carbon and graphite products for flashlight batteries, radio and hearing aids, over 250 synthetic chemicals, alloy steels so much used in industry, plastics and plastic materials made from vinyl resins.

About the turn of the century National Carbon had its headquarters in Cleveland and seven plants in the Middle West. It was at that time that J. S. Crider, Vice President and General Manager, called in F. W. Moses to help him with fire protection and insurance problems. After the organization of Union Carbide in 1917 the headquarters was moved to New York, where the company still maintains its insurance department. After half a century Union Carbide is still insured with us.

## "THE INCORRUPTIBLE CASHIER"

Jᴀᴍᴇꜱ Rɪᴛᴛʏ, a restaurant keeper of Dayton, Ohio, was en route to Europe in the summer of 1878. Observing a revolution counter on the ship's propeller shaft, he became convinced that a machine could be devised to make a record of the money transactions of his business. Thus was born the first cash register. It was called "Ritty's Incorruptible Cashier."

Ritty had little success in marketing his register and in 1881 sold the business to a group which incorporated as the National Manufacturing Company. The cash register as developed by Ritty was merely a recording device; as finally marketed, it had a cash drawer and bell added. It was to be known later as "the bell heard round the world."

In 1883 John H. Patterson, a coal dealer, was so impressed with the savings effected through the use of the cash register in his coal business that he determined to buy the company and by 1884 had acquired control and had changed the name to the National Cash Register Company.

Patterson was essentially a pioneer in sales procedure; he was in fact a generation ahead of his time and was the first in our country to develop for his company the many high-pressure systematic sales programs so usual today.

The basic philosophy of the National Cash sales training is the education of men in detecting those things which happen in a business that result in loss of money, merchandise or manpower. Patterson believed that the only satisfactory selling service consisted in helping the prospect to recognize his business problems, and then helping him to overcome them.

He was greatly impressed with Moses' approach to the fire menace, perhaps because the Factory Mutual methods were so similar to those that Patterson was proving so successful in his own business. Soon his plant was protected in accordance with our standards and insured with us; it remains so after fifty years.

The thirteen original employees of National Cash Register have grown to 17,000; its products are sold throughout the world. Under our guidance no serious fires have occurred to interrupt its progress.

*The original office of the Firemen's was in the building at far left,
facing Market Square in Providence.*

*The entire staff of the Firemen's and the Union companies, except for the
president, posed for this picture in 1894.*

*Pounding hooves and belching smoke mark the flight of the steam pumper.*

# 2

# Years of Expansion

THE ROLL OF GREAT COMPANIES we have served goes on and on—Babcock & Wilcox, who developed the first water tube boiler; United States Playing Card, who converted 52 ordinary pieces of pasteboard with the usual pips into something of beauty and artistic merit; Colgate, founded by William Colgate in 1806 when he made his start peddling laundry soap from door to door in New York, then a city of 84,000; Goodrich, first in the rubber industry, who furnished us with a very helpful director for many years; Larkin of Buffalo, whose sale of soap, with premium attached, stimulated many a small boy to practice his salesmanship on the neighboring housewife; J. I. Case, embarking in the farm implement field. Many an oldster remembers Libbey Glass from the Nineties when the prosperity of the home owner was somewhat measured by the amount of "cut glass" that the ladies could collect. Libbey was later to merge with the brain child of Mike Owens, the inventor of the automatic bottle blowing machine—ancestors of today's Libbey-Owens-Ford. The names of these companies are an endless procession, a Who's Who of American Industry!

The "Senior" Factory Mutual Companies had so far displayed little interest in extending their business. Most of their activities in this respect consisted of raids on the business that had been developed by the "Junior" Companies because such raids required little in the way of effort or expense. However, the Firemen's activities and Moses' success gradually stimulated the managements of the other companies to a realization of the necessity for a more aggressive attitude if they were to maintain their position in the Factory Mutual group.

An idea once established and proved successful has many claimants to its origin. The accomplishments of American industry are seldom the invention of one man. So it was with the Factory Mutuals—Allen, the inventor; Atkinson, the promoter; Freeman, who supplied the engineering; and Moses, whose vision and foresight converted a modest provincial effort into a national institution.

The distinction between "Senior" and "Junior" companies has ceased to have any real importance. Today's group consists of eight companies, the result of the amalgamation over the years of perhaps fifty. Each of the eight is a separate corporation under separate management; each exchanges business with the other seven. For a number of years the "Junior" group maintained a separate Engineering Division in Philadelphia. To all intents and purposes their organization was quite similar to that of the "Senior" group in Boston and, from the standpoint of losses, their experience was fully as good as that of the "Senior" companies. In 1922 the two engineering operations were combined, with laboratories at Norwood, Massachusetts. The present Engineering Division is maintained by all the Factory Mutual companies for the development and adaptation of fire prevention standards, the adjustment of losses and other matters requiring joint effort.

Early in 1912 the Firemen's opened an office in Detroit in collaboration with the Protection Mutual. It was under the management of Moses' son, Frederick T. Moses, the author of this book, and was designed to provide immediate personal service to the growing industries of that section. This was the first of the many branch offices opened by various companies in the Factory Mutual group.

*The old steam pumping engine rides on a motor truck.*

*The gasoline engine wins a race with firehorses.*

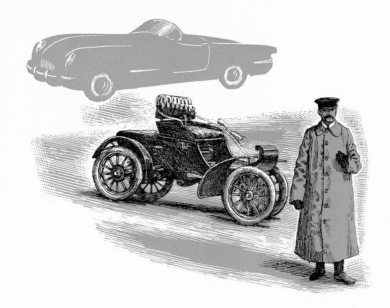

## *"GET A HORSE!"*

Nothing was to make so great a change in the life of America as the automobile; even the briefest chronology would be inadequate without some mention of it.

In the Smithsonian Institution at Washington is what is regarded by that institution as the first automobile. It is the Duryea, built in 1892 by Charles E. Duryea of Springfield, Massachusetts, a mechanic and inventor who, like many others, began his transportation career in the bicycle business. Twenty five hundred other makes were to follow that Duryea.

New England had a long tradition of manufacturing and mechanical ingenuity, and hence it was natural to expect that much of the industry should center in that region. However, more aggressive characters quickly moved it westward, leaving the eastern capitalist, for a few years at least, admiringly contemplating his presumed shrewdness.

By 1904 Detroit was becoming the automobile center and R. E. Olds the acknowledged leader of the industry which many others were to enter at about that time. Leland, with his Cadillac, was the first to develop precision manufacturing and interchangeable parts. Henry Ford had started his career building racing machines; his early ventures were unsuccessful. David Buick, a bathtub manufacturer, built and marketed a car in 1903. The company was a financial failure and about on the verge of bankruptcy when it was rescued by W. C. Durant, an erstwhile carriage manufacturer of Flint, Michigan.

Following his rescue of Buick, Durant, now a wealthy man, proceeded in 1908 to organize General Motors. Like many another company, General Motors expanded so rapidly that its production capacity far exceeded its sales and it found itself without adequate capital. The control passed into other hands and by 1910 Durant was back where he had started.

Meanwhile Ford, having refused Durant's offer to join General Motors, had developed the famous Model T and in 1909 this was put on the market where it was to remain for many years, the supreme accomplishment in cheap transportation. Ford's only important outside connection was with Dodge Brothers. They, like many others, had been bicycle manufacturers but had turned their ingenuity in the direction of automobiles and for several years made the Ford engines, axles and various other parts.

It is hard to put a finger on one specific year, but certainly in 1911 Detroit was humming. General Motors had not only developed a strong centralized organization but its plant managers included two individuals later to become known for their own accomplishments—Walter P. Chrysler and Charles W. Nash. Ford had sold his Detroit plant to Studebaker and had erected a new one in Highland Park. William S. Knudsen, who in later life was to be President of General Motors, was superintendent of a Ford plant established in Buffalo. The Dodge brothers had sold their stock back to the Ford Motor Company and commenced the manufacture of a car of their own. In 1928 Dodge Brothers became part of the Chrysler Corporation, now insured with us.

41

The more farsighted automobile manufacturers realized the importance of protecting their properties. There were too many competitors in the industry to take a chance of fire causing a shutdown.

The insurance of General Motors, Ford, Studebaker, Dodge Brothers and many other now less well-known names was therefore placed through the Firemen's-Protection office. It was a period of intense activity. Ford was building assembly plants all over the country; his immense undertaking at River Rouge was under way. General Motors and others had substantial construction projects.

When World War I came, the automobile industry found itself supplying trucks, guns, airplane motors, even Eagle boats. Many problems arose overnight. There was no experienced fire-protection engineering immediately available from insurance sources except through our office. Not only during that period but through a second world war, indeed for over a generation, that part of the automobile industry protected in accordance with our standards and kept under our supervision has never suffered a seriously crippling fire.

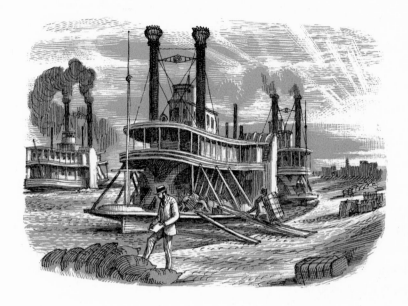

## IT'S IN THE BAG

O<small>F ALL THE</small> ordinary articles that touch our everyday life, who ever stops to think of the history of the bag?

In 1836 a Massachusetts chair maker named Bemis loaded his family into a covered wagon and finally settled in Lighthouse Point, Illinois. The younger son, Judson Bemis, in his early days was employed as a clerk with a firm of shipping agents at an initial salary of $250 per year. A permanent career as a shipping clerk did not appeal to the ambitious Judson; he decided that opportunity might lie in the production of bags for the milling industry, much of which centered about St. Louis.

Thereupon in 1858 he invested his life savings of $2,000; a cousin supplied six sewing machines, two small printing presses and some wooden type; Judson rented space for the new company in the second story of

43

a small stone building in St. Louis—and Bemis Bag was in business.

All the bags of that era had been hand-sewn and the trade naturally viewed Judson's new machine-made product with suspicion. To overcome it, he guaranteed every bag and the product soon demonstrated its quality and toughness. Business increased in St. Louis, but Judson wanted out-of-town business. How could he find his sales prospects in a day when there were no directories, no trade journals? He went down to the levees, by the old river steamboat landings and, pencil in hand, copied the stenciled names of millers and other shippers off the piled bags of cargo.

The histories of all great and successful American industries seem to have one development in common, namely, the control of the production of raw materials. So with Bemis—eventually it acquired its own cotton mills and bleacheries, a plant to make ink, a machine works to manufacture special bag-making machinery and printing presses, the control of the output of a jute mill in Calcutta. As the use of wooden containers decreased, it became necessary to develop an especially tough brand of paper, not then commercially available. In 1913, therefore, Bemis built its own paper mill.

Perhaps one of the most interesting products is the feed store bag made of a printed cotton that the thrifty housewife can salvage and turn into anything from a gay blouse to a kitchen curtain. This product has been intelligently promoted by having the designs approved by a statewide committee of women and, in turn, developing a special ink so that the label can be readily washed out. Certainly the first Bemis would never have dreamed of a pretty girl attired in a bathing suit made from a Bemis feed bag.

The Bemis Bro. Bag Company is now the world's largest bag manufacturer, producing many products as diverse as open-mesh orange bags, tents, tarpaulins, mattress bags and coffin covers. The company realizes that the bags must be there when the contents are ready, and is aware of the importance of avoiding a serious fire, with its possible loss of production. For over half a century Bemis Bag's connection with us has assured it comparative immunity from fire.

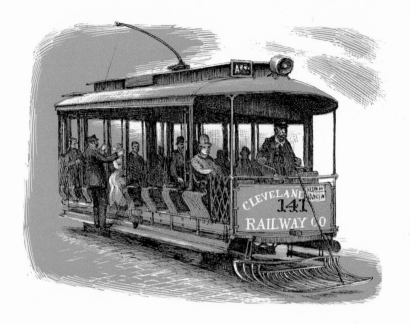

## THREE CENTS A RIDE

IN 1912 CLEVELAND, OHIO, was outstanding in the field of electric street car transportation. Following a stormy political battle the street railway company had secured from the city an agreement designated as the Taylor Franchise, whereby the earnings of the company were on a guaranteed 6% basis and the rate of fare was allowed to vary to assure such earnings. The fare at that time was three cents!! Such was the wisdom and foresight of this agreement that the Cleveland Railway Company became the best managed and best maintained of the large trolley systems of the country.

Insurance rates were high and there was no competition. The street railways of the country, through their national association, had organized their own insurance company but it was not large enough to be of any help. While a street car burned occasionally from well-recognized hazards, the principal fear of the management was that a fire might occur at night when the cars were out of service and there were large concentrations of value in car barns and storage yards.

The Firemen's Detroit office was called in and asked to study the problem and find a way to bring this business up to Factory Mutual standards. Automatic sprinklers had been provided in the car barns but they could not throw any water inside the car body where fires usually occurred. In the mammoth car storage yards hose could not be laid across the tracks because it might be cut.

After numerous tests we provided for aisle sprinklers in the barns between each line of cars where they could operate through the windows. In the car yards monitor nozzles, such as had been devised for the protection of pulp wood piles, were fixed to the tops of poles and supplied from an electrically driven fire pump with a starting switch on each nozzle. Thus an employee could quickly climb the ladder to the top of a pole and direct a stream at a burning car before it could involve others. In the meantime, it was found that the two principal internal causes of car fires were the un-insulated heating stoves and the unprotected resistance grids, very minor deficiencies easily and quickly corrected. When newer cars were designed, their motors were enclosed in cast iron housings so that even in the event of fire the loss was limited to the bodies, which represented only 40% of the value.

Thus was the problem solved and oh, how quickly the stock company rate was dropped!

Other street railways followed the example of Cleveland but as time went on electric railways were discontinued or, as in Cleveland's case, replaced by gasoline buses; the business decreased until now its volume is comparatively small.

After 42 years we still carry the insurance of the Cleveland Railway Company even though it operates no more street cars.

## THE PRACTICAL GENIUS

Thomas A. Edison was and still is a household word. It is said that he was responsible for over 2000 inventions, some of which constitute the beginning of many of our outstanding industries.

Edison's genius lay in making things work. Certainly among the many contributors to scientific and technical advancement in his time, no individual had a greater impact on the modern world. His importance rests not only on the invention of an astounding multitude of devices but also on the fact that he created the first substantial laboratory in the world devoted exclusively to converting inventive ideas into practical products.

"Genius," said Edison, "is two per cent inspiration and 98 per cent perspiration." He spent ten years working to perfect his storage battery and made 50,000 experiments before he was satisfied with it. Today the storage battery is one of the principal products of the company which bears his name.

In 1928, when the U. S. Congress awarded him its gold medal, it placed a value of $15,599,000,000 on his contributions to humanity. But the commercial value of his various inventions bore only chance relation to the effort that went into them. As a young man he invented a stock ticker and sold it at once for $40,000. Again he labored to perfect a vote-counting device for legislative bodies, only to learn that the last thing legislators wanted was a machine to speed up their voting. It took him only a year to produce the incandescent electric light, complete with plans for central power stations, transmission lines and lighting systems for homes and cities. On the other hand, he tinkered for 34 years with his "kinetoscope," and even synchronized it with his phonograph to make talking motion pictures—yet never thought of the device as much more than a peep-show toy.

Sometimes the inventor's imagination skipped one whole stage in the application of a device and fixed on the next stage. When he invented the phonograph Edison foresaw but dimly its popularity as a medium of music and entertainment. But he clearly envisaged its use as a business machine, with "the businessman reclining at ease on a couch and smoking a cigar as he speaks into the instrument." Today the Edison Voicewriter is another principal product of Thomas A. Edison, Inc.

Like many men of this type, Edison was too preoccupied to think of the fire hazard, with the result that his company suffered a serious fire in 1914. Surveying the ruins the next morning, the great man said, "I'm 67 years old but not too old to make a fresh start tomorrow morning. No one is ever too old to make a fresh start." Within three weeks the company was operating again, this time with a healthy respect for the risk of fire. Efforts to solve the fire protection problem through usual channels were not satisfactory, however, and in 1922 Thomas A. Edison, Inc. came to us; it has been with us ever since.

*Thomas Edison (left) shows off an old mill wheel to three famous friends:*
*John Burroughs, Henry Ford and Harvey Firestone.*

This fire which destroyed the Firestone rubber factory in New Bedford, Mass., in 1941, was a severe blow to the war effort. The author witnessed this blaze from his yacht, which was then serving in the Coast Guard Auxiliary.

# 3

# New Fields for the Firemen's

THE COMPANY WAS GROWING so rapidly that in 1920 your historian, Frederick T. Moses, was called back to Providence to assume the duties of Executive Vice President and, because of his father's impaired health, took over most of the executive direction of the company.

As a means of establishing a connection in the South the Firemen's in April, 1922, assumed the management of the Baltimore Mutual Fire Insurance Company. F. W. Moses was elected President; Frederick T. Moses, Executive Vice President, took charge of this company.

The Baltimore had been incorporated in 1885 and was originally known as the Fertilizer Manufacturers Mutual Fire Insurance Company. The name was then changed to the Mutual Fire Insurance Company of Baltimore City, but this was found awkward and was soon changed again to Baltimore Mutual Fire Insurance Company. About 1904 the Patapsco Mutual Fire Insurance Company was incorporated and a few years later the Maryland Mutual Fire Insurance Company. All three were managed by the same group of officers and directors. The arrangement was cumbersome and they were soon merged into one company, the Baltimore.

It is of interest that in the beginning most of the organizers and directors of these companies were men affiliated with the fertilizer and chemical industry. Since its loss experience with the fertilizer industry was unsatisfactory, the management of the Baltimore decided to transfer its efforts to the textile industry. This was before the days of the Factory Insurance Association and the stock companies were represented in the Southern territory by the Southeastern Underwriters Association. Their methods were highhanded and their rates excessive; consequently the relief afforded by the mutual companies was most welcome. To the question of who founded Factory Mutual Insurance in the South, an effective answer may be found in the list of the Baltimore directors:

William H. Purcell, *President of the Baltimore Company*

Summerfield Baldwin, Sr., *President, Warren Manufacturing Co., Baltimore, Maryland*

William K. Cromwell, *Vice President, Mount Vernon-Woodberry Cotton Duck Co.*

John W. Chafee, *President, The Sibley Manufacturing Co., Augusta, Georgia*

A. S. Hamilton, *President, Trion Manufacturing Co., Trion Factory, Georgia*

A. H. Twitchell, *President, *Clifton Manufacturing Co., Clifton, S. C.*

Ellison A. Smyth, *President, *Pelzer Manufacturing Co., Pelzer, S. C.*

H. D. Wheat, *President, *Gaffney Manufacturing Co., Gaffney, S. C.*

John H. Montgomery, *President, *Sparton and *Pacolet Mills, Spartanburg, S. C.*

James L. Orr, *President, *Piedmont Manufacturing Co., Greenville, S. C.*

J. A. Brock, *President, Anderson Cotton Mills, Anderson, S. C.*

Leroy Springs, *President, The Lancaster Cotton Mills, Lancaster, S. C.*

T. J. McCrary, *President, The Newberry Cotton Mills, Newberry, S. C.*

Robert D. Hopkins, *Treasurer, Brigham-Hopkins, Baltimore, Maryland*

* Still insured with the Factory Mutuals.

They were not just dummy directors; they attended the meetings and took an active interest in promoting the company.

The Baltimore was burned out in the famous conflagration of 1904 and lost all of its records. As a result of this calamity and the constant raids on its business by the "Senior" Companies, it had reached a point at the time we took it over where its business had shrunk to a very modest volume. Among the few large accounts, it had retained the business of the West Virginia Pulp & Paper Company whose president, David Luke, had continued as a director.

After an experience of eighteen months, the management came to the conclusion that the maintenance of so small a unit as a separate company was an unwarranted expense. So, in October, 1923 the Firemen's reinsured the business of the Baltimore and transferred all its operations to Providence.

In 1922 Frederick T. Moses took over the management of the Mercantile and Narragansett Mutual Fire Insurance Companies, two members of the "Junior" Group that were organized in 1884 and 1894 respectively. We maintained them as separate companies until 1934 when, as a matter of operating economy, they were reinsured and merged with the Firemen's.

Among the Mercantile accounts there were three that today seem to have especial historical interest; they are the Bibb Manufacturing Company, the R. J. Reynolds Tobacco Company and the Eastman Kodak Company.

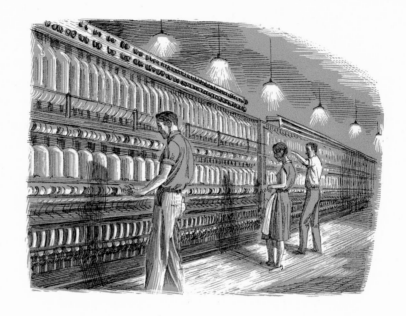

## *"THE BIBB"*

I<small>T WAS TWELVE YEARS</small> after Sherman's devastating march through Georgia, the Ku Klux Klan was riding high, kerosene illuminated the American home. Three enterprising cotton buyers, Major J. F. Hanson and his brother, of Macon, Georgia and H. M. Comer of Savannah, Georgia, decided to go into the textile industry. They possessed a charter permitting them to sell "grits," meal and flour, a capital of $35,000 and a building which had successively served as a freight warehouse, schoolhouse and grist mill. The charter was elastic and the milling operation helped to provide current funds. There remained the choosing of a name. Macon is located in Bibb County which was named after a popular figure who had been prominent in Georgia politics, afterward reaching the zenith of his career as the first Governor of Alabama, one Dr. Bibb. Thus was born the Bibb Manufacturing Company, then and now known locally as "The Bibb."

The new company prospered; consequently five years later it was able to acquire additional capital by selling 350 shares of stock to a Liverpool firm of cotton merchants at $237.50 per share. During the next forty years other mills were acquired in different parts of the State and combined into a single organization. Their products have changed with the times—they range from the twine for industry and for the nets of the fishermen to soft goods for the housewife; nearly every cotton article today could be one of their products.

Prior to 1917 automobile tires used a plain woven canvas base. They were guaranteed for 3000 miles; frequently they didn't go that far. In 1917 Goodyear produced the first cord tire in the United States made with a fabric known as Hawser Cord, a development of "The Bibb." While the new tires were a substantial improvement, there was still much tire trouble due primarily to overheating. After several years of painstaking research "The Bibb" came forth with a new and hitherto unknown material, a truly heat-resistant cord. The product so defied all formerly known standards of testing, as prescribed by "the book" of the Bureau of Standards, that the textbooks in use by the cotton industry had to be rewritten. Today's tire cord is fundamentally the same except that it is mostly made of rayon. The motorist of the present, with thousands of miles on his set of tires, can well appreciate "The Bibb"—especially if he is old enough to have had to struggle with the early product.

Much of World War II was the war of the airplane. Parachute harnesses had always been made of linen; no other fabric was considered to possess the requisite tensile strength. When shipments of linen from abroad were cut off, "The Bibb" was asked by the armed forces to develop a cotton substitute. The substitute was so good that it exceeded all strength requirements for linen as prescribed by the Bureau of Standards—another accomplishment of American industry.

Our connection with "The Bibb" goes back to 1894; indeed, we believe it to be one of the first, if not the first, Factory Mutual risk in the South.

From their humble beginning in 1876 with 2500 spindles, the mills today have over 250,000; the number of employees has grown to 7500. In an industry that for over thirty years has been beset with endless difficulties, Bibb stands out as one that has been conspicuously successful. Dividends have been paid to stockholders without interruption since 1887. How many in the textile industry can equal that record?

Your historian believes that a business, like an individual, possesses an accumulation of traditions resulting in a certain philosophy of life. Perhaps that of "The Bibb" is contained in this quotation from its Executive Vice President, Archie A. Drake:

> "Down through the ages, Business has been but another name for the struggle to exist. Its broad law has been the 'survival of the fittest.'
>
> "Buy, manufacture, and sell have been common terms since the days of Tubal-cain; and legion are the tales of trickery by which one man has advantaged himself over another of a lesser shrewdness. Laban, the Syrian, has had his counterpart in every community since barter began.
>
> "But there might also be cited countless instances of love and kindness in the world of trade. Friendship has played a leading part in this huge drama, among those upright citizens of whatever country who place honor before profit. Not every great fortune has been amassed through an unworthy seizure of a Naboth's vineyard."

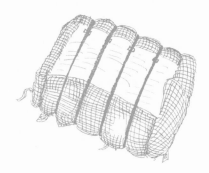

## "OLD JOE" AND THE CIGARETTE

Wᴇ ʀᴇᴀᴅ ᴛʜᴀᴛ Cᴀᴍᴇʟ is the largest selling cigarette; not all of us know how it got its name. When this cigarette was born and waiting to be christened the circus came to town and Reynolds Tobacco was closed for a holiday. The circus had two camels—one with two humps, another with one. A local photographer took pictures of both. The one-humper, known as Old Joe, was chosen, the palm trees and pyramid dubbed in; Old Joe survives on billions of packets.

Most of our thinking today concerning tobacco companies is in terms of cigarettes, yet, when the Reynolds Tobacco Company was formed, in 1875, and as late as 1906, chewing tobacco made up 98% of the sales.

In 1899 R. J. Reynolds joined his company with James B. Duke's vast American Tobacco Company, where he was frequently considered a somewhat undigested unit. At any rate, when the "Tobacco Trust" was dissolved by the Supreme Court in 1911, the Reynolds Company happily resumed its original independent status.

In 1913 Reynolds began the manufacture of Camels, the first cigarette to be composed of the modern blend of Virginia bright leaf, Kentucky burley and Turkish, the first to be distributed on a national basis. In World War I our service men in Europe popularized them throughout the world. Today cigarettes represent about 93% of the Reynolds output.

The development of the cigarette brought with it a fire protection problem. Cigarette tobacco cannot be used immediately but requires aging for two years. That means many millions of dollars tied up in tobacco storage. When fire comes, it also means the destruction of a product which is, because of its age, practically irreplaceable. Much thought and care had been given to this situation by the Reynolds management, who called upon us for a solution of their fire prevention problem. Their vast and valuable storage areas were subdivided and protected according to our standards. Result: only one important storage fire in many years and that one was incendiary.

## *"YOU PRESS THE BUTTON,*
## *WE DO THE REST"*

O<small>F THE NUMEROUS</small> corporations insured by the Mercantile when we assumed its management none illustrates more clearly how the vision and enterprise of one man built an enormous industry than the story of the Eastman Kodak Company.

George Eastman was an office boy in an insurance firm, his formal education having stopped at fourteen. Some of the ideas behind photography date back somewhere near the 16th century, but no great progress was made until the 19th, and the first actual photographs were taken in the 1830's and 1840's. When Eastman purchased his first photographic outfit in 1877, practitioners of the art were held in disrepute or viewed with humorous indulgence, apparatus was bulky and complicated.

Eastman's first efforts led to the invention of a method for the mass production of emulsion-coated glass plates. Having secured some financial backing, he gave up his job as bookkeeper in a bank and organized the Eastman Dry Plate Company in 1880.

During the next few years he was to conduct many experiments with various materials, resulting in 1899 in the introduction of the first commercial transparent roll film. This could be loaded only in a dark room but it soon gave way to the daylight loading roll film, somewhat as we know it today. This was first marketed in 1891.

Although roll film holders were now available for plate cameras, they were not a satisfactory product to put into the hands of the general public, so in 1888 Eastman's first box camera was placed on the market and the name "Kodak" registered as a trade mark. This camera was sold already loaded with sufficient film for 100 exposures. After exposure the whole was returned to Rochester where the film was removed and processed and the camera re-loaded. Some of us are old enough to remember the slogan that went along with that beginning—"You Press the Button, We Do the Rest."

Eastman was still in pursuit of the mass market and in 1900, with his famous $1 Brownie Camera, he found it.

The fire hazards of the business were severe. Film was made from nitrated cotton, the "gun cotton" of the explosive world; furthermore, the solvents used were necessarily highly inflammable. Numerous fires involving the finished product in the hands of the public were to emphasize its dangers. Eastman himself fully realized this and we were brought into the picture, our first inspection having been made in 1903.

The nitration of the cotton was a comparatively small unit and quite readily segregated. The danger of the product itself was sometimes demonstrated to the insurance visitor with a handful on the ground—a match—whoosh!!

The film was coated, then dried in the dark in festoons several hundred feet long. It was so highly inflammable that the ordinary sprinkler system was too slow. To cope with this we developed a much more sensitive pre-action system, and the drying cells were separated into many small units. An elaborate system of vaults was constructed under our supervision for the storage of the finished product. Our solution of their many other fire protection problems was facilitated by the cooperative attitude of Eastman and the unusually able executive staff with which he had surrounded himself.

The danger was eventually to be removed in another way. In 1908 the first safe film was manufactured, using cellulose acetate. There were to be many years of research before this could be made commercially practical, but at the end of 1950 the manufacture of the highly inflammable nitrate film was permanently discontinued.

It is perhaps natural to pick out a danger spot and highlight it, but Kodak has had many ramifications. The Camera Works is a marvel of precision manufacturing. The plant at Kingsport, Tennessee, manufacturing solvents and the cellulose acetate base, has extended its operations to the manufacture of acetate yarn and fibre, plastics and chemicals. The Distillation Products division, which began as a research project, is now a whole new industry engaged in the manufacture of high vacuum equipment and vitamins. Gelatin is a vital ingredient in film manufacture and is produced by the Eastman Gelatin Company in Peabody, Massachusetts.

X-Ray film, moving picture film, micro-filming of records, color processes efficient even in the hands of amateurs, endless complicated equipment—what an accomplishment to spring from Eastman's original third-floor loft and five-man staff!

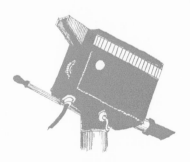

FREDERICK TAFT MOSES
*President of the Firemen's, 1926-1951, Chairman of the Board since 1951.*

# 4

# Under New Leadership

F. W. MOSES RETIRED as President in 1926 and died in 1928. We who were associated with him lost a good friend and a wise leader, his thinking many years ahead of that of his contemporaries. During his administration the gross business of the Firemen's had increased from $9 million to over $800 million.

His son, Frederick T. Moses, who succeeded him, was born in Ayer, Massachusetts, November 14, 1885. He was educated in the public schools of Ayer and Fitchburg, Massachusetts, and graduated from Massachusetts Institute of Technology in the class of 1907.

He was superintendent of Taylor & Barker Chemical Company, a wood distilling plant near Lowell, Massachusetts; superintendent of the Talbot Dyewood & Chemical Company, North Billerica, Massachusetts, and later in charge of the research department of the MacBeth Evans Glass Company, Pittsburgh, Pennsylvania. He came with the Firemen's in 1911 as Assistant Secretary, after a year in the Inspection Department. In 1912 he was transferred to our newly established Detroit office, and elected Vice President in 1915. He returned to Providence in 1920 as

Executive Vice President. He was elected President in February, 1926.

Under his leadership, and following our consolidation of the Firemen's with the Baltimore, Mercantile and Narragansett Companies, we embarked upon a vigorous program of business development.

An office had been opened in New York in 1921 and the Detroit office was moved to Cleveland in 1924. As time went on other locations were established. All of this resulted in the partial decentralization of our business and was so successful that during the next twenty years most of the other Factory Mutual Companies followed our lead.

The depression of the early 30's imposed a serious financial problem on the entire insurance industry. The Dow Jones average dropped from 381 in 1929 to 41 in 1932 and there existed a constant fear that in the event of a serious fire loss it might become necessary to sell securities in the depressed market to realize needed cash.

The simplest and most immediate protection was to purchase what is termed excess conflagration insurance from London Lloyd's, and this the Firemen's and other Factory Mutual Companies proceeded to do. A great deal of bewilderment existed in the minds of the managements of the Factory Mutuals unused to this form of coverage. But because of our experience with such contracts in our related company, the Union Mutual (see Chapter V), we in the Firemen's were able to come to their rescue and establish a satisfactory relationship with Lloyd's that still exists.

Our conflagration insurance was first to be called upon following the hurricane of September 21, 1938, an occurrence which is still a landmark in our local history, since New England, like many other sections of the country, was considered practically immune to this type of disturbance.

A wind velocity of 121 miles per hour, reaching its maximum just at the top of the unusually high tide common to the autumnal equinox, caused a tidal wave resulting in some ten feet of water in the streets of downtown Providence. Similar conditions prevailed to a greater or less degree in many other New England seacoast communities. In many places fire followed wind and flood. Roads were blocked by trees, communications were cut off, there was no light, heat or power. Our millions of dollars'

*Ten feet of water flooded the heart of Providence during the hurricane of 1938, marooning street cars and completely covering automobiles.*

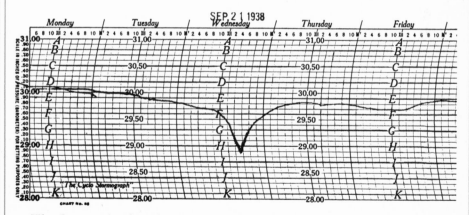

*The Barograph Chart for the week of the hurricane shows a drop to 28.9 inches on September 21, the most precipitous drop in New England records.*

worth of securities stored in bank vaults were soaked with gummy sea water. Immediately followed a vast scurrying to purchase old-fashioned flatirons, oil stoves and blotting paper. Some of our young women washed, dried and pressed mightily for several days (none of the millions rubbed off), surrounded by two-gun guards—one humorous compensation for the daily climbing of nine flights of stairs.

In the New England area some 588 lives were lost, and total property damage was reported to be over $500 million, most of it without insurance protection. The element of unawareness caused much of the loss of life and the feeling which existed that "it can't happen here" was responsible for the lack of insurance.

Owing to the enterprise of the Firemen's and its Factory Mutual Associates, however, those fortunate enough to be insured with our companies were compensated in full for their windstorm property losses. Windstorm insurance, with various modifications, had been included in Factory Mutual policies since 1913, and in more recent years with no additional premium charge—a procedure eventually followed by our competitors.

A cyclonic type of storm occurred on November 25, 1950, and two severe tornadoes hit the Flint, Michigan, and Worcester, Massachusetts, areas on June 8 and 9, 1953. In fact the windstorm losses of 1953 have been the greatest in the history of the entire insurance industry.

These occurrences and a few fire losses which involved the Lloyd's coverage justify the wisdom of the management.

In the history of a business good times may show the most spectacular gains but hard times provide the real test. The depression of the early 30's was an anxious time for all insurance companies; during this period the Firemen's was one of the few companies that continued to prosper.

By the time the depression had passed much of our development work had been completed, and our company and the methods which had made it so successful were nationally recognized and continuously imitated. Many new and now well-known industries were to turn to us for a solution of their insurance and fire protection problems. In a brief chronology such as this we can mention but a few.

The 1953 tornado cut this path of total destruction through Worcester, Mass.
At left, the Housing Authority development, insured by the Firemen's, was
damaged but not destroyed.

## *ROBOTS FOR SILKWORMS*

In 1870 THE EVERYDAY GARMENTS of the young lady of fashion consisted of some forty yards of linen, cotton, wool and silk, enough to make
a suit of sails for a sloop. Silk especially was a luxury fabric, the use of
which was limited mostly to the wealthy.

Today the silkworm has succumbed to science and the modern housewife is modestly and fashionably dressed in just about five yards of almost
weightless material.

The history of synthetic fiber goes back to the 17th century, but it
remained merely a scientific curiosity until the 1880's when a "silk" was
produced on a commercial scale in France. Unfortunately it was a nitro-
cellulose product, burning furiously, and following a number of painful
incidents its manufacture was prohibited by law.

Two English chemists finally produced a safe product and their process, discovered in 1892, got underway commercially in 1905. The manufacture of rayon is, in effect, a mechanical imitation of the silkworm. The ingenious creature feeds on mulberry leaves, which it chews and digests into a viscous mass of cellulose. Then, through two tiny holes in the top of its head, the worm extrudes a pair of long filaments, winding them around and around its body to make the cocoon. The manufacture of rayon begins with wood pulp, which is "digested" by chemicals into a clear amber syrup. This viscose is then extruded through a spinneret which serves the same purpose as the silkworm's head except that, instead of two tiny holes, it has a hundred or more.

American Viscose built the first commercially successful rayon plant in the United States in 1910. It is, indeed, the father of our rayon industry. In addition to making fibers for clothing of all descriptions, it produces cellophane for wrappings, cord for our tires and synthetic materials that go into miscellaneous products from tea bags to carpets—over one-third of all the man-made fibers produced in the United States.

We protect and insure the eight plants of American Viscose; we protect the jobs of 20,000 employees; we protect the investment of 17,000 stockholders.

## *AMERICAN WOOL FOR WASHINGTON*

In Babylon as early as 4000 B.C., man had learned the arts of spinning and weaving by hand and was wearing woolen garments. The spinning wheel was to develop in India forty centuries later and, after another 1500 years, Leonardo da Vinci improved the wheel so that in one continuous motion it twisted the yarn and wound it onto the bobbin. Three hundred years later, in the 18th century, da Vinci's spinning wheel inspired Richard Arkwright's spinning frame and James Hargreaves' spinning jenny, both adapted to wool. Originally the power for these machines was furnished by horses, later by water wheels and eventually by steam engines.

American textile manufacturing was slow in starting because the British refused to permit the export of textile machinery. Sheep were unknown to the North American Indian, and the early colonists brought in only a few;

thereafter the British refused to export sheep to the Colonies. Eventually a few sheep were imported from France and Spain, and adventurous men memorized specifications for textile machinery well enough so that they could build machinery, by hand, in America. Thus in 1788 the first United States woolen mill got its start in Hartford, Connecticut. By the following spring a few yards of the new mill's best cloth could be sent to New York and made into George Washington's first inaugural suit.

New England was the home of the industry, and a few companies in Lawrence, Massachusetts, became the key mills around which the huge American Woolen Company was built in 1899. Just before its formation, the woolen industry was in a chaotic condition. Manufacturing was carried on in small, separate mills often operated by families with fierce pride in their own standards and products.

One man was to stand out as the manufacturing genius of the industry— William E. Wood, a young man from Martha's Vineyard. It was he who had the driving ability to attract the necessary capital and put through the original combination, until 27 mills had entered and the American Woolen Company was established. By the time of World War I the corporation had a total of fifty mills and 10,000 looms. Even this tremendous productive capacity could not meet the orders that were coming in.

Following the war conditions changed and during the "Roaring Twenties," when the nation was enjoying prosperity, the woolen industry was in the doldrums. Many factors entered into this: there was fierce competition from other fibers, there was over-production, there was a demand for a wider variety of fabrics and colors in men's clothing. This chapter might be termed the "end of the blue serge." Especially notable was the change in women's wardrobes: as moralists and industrialists noted with equal horror, women were wearing less and less—and less. World War II brought another period of prosperity, lasting through 1951. But with the collapse of this latest boom, trouble again overtook American Woolen.

Much of the fire protection of the individual mills had been planned by the Factory Mutuals. We in the Firemen's were called upon to coordinate and combine both fire protection and insurance for the entire group.

## *FAMOUS NAMES IN FOOD*

In 1892 one Charles W. Post bought a farm in Battle Creek, Michigan, and after two years' experimentation with grain combinations came forth in 1895 with the first Postum cereal, to be followed in later years by the many Post products now so well known.

Even earlier, in 1845, Peter Cooper, inventor of the famous locomotive "Tom Thumb," secured the first patent for a gelatin dessert. Nothing was done with it, the business passed into other hands, and it was not until about 1900 that the now famous Jell-O caught on with the public and became a success. In 1925 Postum Cereal and Jell-O combined to form the nucleus of what is now the General Foods Corporation.

In 1856 Levi Igleheart started a gristmill in Evansville, Indiana. When the business passed to his three sons, Addison, who was especially fond of cake, decided that his wife's cooking would be improved if he could develop a fine, low gluten flour specifically designed for cake. Thus was born the famous Swans Down, joined with General Foods in 1926.

As time went on many diverse products were to round out the General Foods organization: Minute Tapioca, which originated because somebody learned to run the coarse cassava flakes through a coffee mill; coconut products because of Franklin Baker, who unwillingly acquired a cargo of coconuts in settlement of a debt; chocolate thanks to Walter Baker, who financed the first chocolate mill in the new world in 1765 and originated the famous trade mark "La Belle Chocolatiere" on the labels of the cakes we used to steal from our mothers.

The Maxwell House Hotel in Nashville was one of the most famous of the old Southern hotels, whose guests included the elite of the land; it gave its name to the famous brand of coffee. In 1944 General Foods research produced one of the first of the well-known instant coffees bearing the same name.

Clarence Birdseye, a Gloucester scientist, spent three years in Labrador buying furs and making a biological survey. He noticed that meat and fish frozen in the Arctic air were still good when cooked months later. On his return home he developed, after several years' experimentation, a quick freezing method which became commercially practical and was sold to General Foods in 1929. Nothing has done more to change the buying habits of the American housewife than frozen foods. The development of frozen concentrates has leveled out the feast and famine industry of the citrus fruit farmer.

General Seafoods, which has its own vessels and freezing plants and now processes over 150 million pounds of fish annually, was a natural corollary to the development of the Birdseye Division. Certo gelatin, coffee with the caffeine removed, nuts, and fruit juices are only a few of the innumerable food products so well known today. Even the production of dog food is determined by nutritional experiments carried out in a research kennel with some two hundred dogs.

Until the beginning of the 19th century nine out of ten persons in

America spent all of their working lives producing and distributing food. It is only through the development of modern methods of processing and distributing foods—only through the enterprise of such leaders of the industry as General Foods—that millions of people are left free to do other kinds of work: to build our automobiles, television sets and refrigerators, and to provide the many other services and luxuries unknown to our forefathers.

Time is of the essence in the food industry. The crop, be it animal or vegetable, must be processed when it is ready. Nothing is so important to General Foods as the assurance of continuity of operation; its many years' connection with our company serves to furnish that assurance.

## *HOUSING BY THE BILLION*

T<small>HE</small> <small>ESTABLISHMENT</small> of the United States Housing Authority of 1937 made Federal funds and credit available to assist the several states and their political subdivisions in slum clearance programs and in the construction of modern low-rent dwelling facilities.

When the Housing Authority was set up there were transferred to it 52 complete properties which had been built by the Public Works Administration of the Department of the Interior. These properties were insured for some $52,000,000 at a three-year insurance cost of $181,000. It was immediately obvious that the cost of insurance was to be an important item in the make-up of the rents of future projects, $800,000,000 of which were authorized by the 1937 Act. The title was changed to Federal Housing Authority (generally referred to as the F.H.A.); it was again

75

changed and is now known as the Public Housing Administration.

Unable to secure assistance from the insurance facilities available, Nathan Straus, the first Administrator, telephoned to ask us to send someone to Washington to see if we could find a way to consider their insurance problem. At first it did not seem to us that this type of property was such that the Firemen's could handle it within the framework of the Factory Mutual system, but after discussing the matter with some of the technical advisors of the Housing Administration we learned that the scope of the control to be exercised by the Authority was such that our requirements regarding construction and protection could be observed. Furthermore, it developed that the proposed volume of property value was so great that we could establish a separate classification for the business and that it could in time stand on its own feet.

Preliminary treatment of the $52,000,000 of property already in existence resulted in our effecting a reduction in the insurance cost for three years from $181,000 to some $48,000.

Since 1937, by careful planning in cooperation with the technical staff of the Authority, and by continued inspection service, we have developed construction and maintenance specifications which are now applied to a billion dollars' worth of these projects. Our experience has justified a further reduction of nearly 50% in our own rates, the competitive market has been prodded into a belated awakening, and the Firemen's marks up another high spot in its career in the conservation of life and property.

The Factory Mutual Laboratory at Norwood, Mass., here framed in smoke from a test, is the only institution in the world devoted exclusively to the study and development of industrial fire protection.

Constant tests are carried out at Norwood. At left, carbon dioxide equipment quenches an oil fire in ten seconds. At right, an oil-filled transformer is ignited to test special water spray nozzles.

*A brave fire laddie of the last century answers the call of duty.*

# 5

# Past and Present

In our story of the Firemen's growth through the years we have passed over several important subjects which have no fixed place in a chronological narrative. Because they are part of our company history they deserve attention in this account.

Through the years the Firemen's has had a close relation with the Union Mutual Fire Insurance Company, which operates outside the field of factory protection. This connection owes its origin to one John Eddy, who was one of the founders of both companies.

Eddy graduated from Brown University in 1840, studied law and eventually settled in Providence. A considerable portion of his practice consisted of insurance cases, in which field he established a wide reputation. Meanwhile, despite his many other business activities, he became one of the founders of the Firemen's and its Secretary. He was also instrumental in launching the Blackstone and Merchants, of which he was President. His son, Alfred U. Eddy, was later to organize the Mercantile and Narragansett Mutual Fire Insurance Companies, of which Alfred was the President at the time of their acquisition by the Firemen's.

John Eddy became interested in the possibilities of organizing a mutual company for the purpose of insuring dwelling houses exclusively, at that time a new departure in the business of fire insurance. With this in mind he caused the organization of the Union Mutual in 1864. During its entire history the Union Mutual has been managed by officers of the Firemen's.

The Factory Mutuals were frequently hampered in their early operations by a lack of facilities for insuring non-factory properties belonging to their policyholders such as small warehouses, branch retail stores and other types of risk which it was not practical to protect in accordance with Factory Mutual standards. To close this gap, the Union in 1928 undertook to insure outside properties of Firemen's policyholders, a first effort to supply some intelligent form of "package" fire insurance. Our eventual success in this field stimulated the Factory Mutual group to organize in 1948 the Affiliated F M Insurance Company, which is now available to all Factory Mutual policyholders.

● ● ●

In the early decades of their history, the Factory Mutuals built up a great store of knowledge about the problem of fire prevention. This knowledge found its initial application in the control of industrial fires. But before the end of the last century there came an opportunity for the Factory Mutuals to make an important contribution to the growing problems of fire prevention in the community at large.

The population of the United States had been rising fast and in its train this growth brought a headlong building boom. Municipal building codes were frequently unavailable and mostly inadequate. There was little regulation of the handling and storage of dangerous materials. The use of electricity was growing rapidly, without too much attention being paid to its hazards. Laws and ordinances necessary for the enforcement of safety regulations were haphazard or non-existent. Because of this situation, loss of life and property was on the increase.

In 1895 a small group of men met in Boston at the instigation of U. C. Crosby, Chairman of the Factory Improvement Committee of the New

England Insurance Exchange. John R. Freeman represented the Factory Mutuals. As a result the National Fire Protection Association was organized in 1896, its original members consisting mostly of insurance men. Technical committees were appointed to develop standards of fire protection and a system was inaugurated to collect and classify fire experience information. The Factory Mutuals supplied most of the background of the technical regulations on which the new organization put its own label, they consisted principally of the fire protection standards which had been developed by Atkinson, Freeman, and their associates. In 1901 the National Board of Fire Underwriters undertook the publication of these N.F.P.A. standards—a practice still partially in existence.

Time is the test of any public service and, over the years, the N.F.P.A. has grown and prospered, if that term can be used in connection with a non-profit organization. It is today an international voluntary association of some 15,000 members, interested in the reduction of loss of life and property by fire; it operates as a worldwide clearing house of information and public education close to the grass roots.

The Factory Mutuals have lent their support to this organization from the beginning, furnishing key members of its technical committees, as well as many of its directors and three of its presidents—H. O. Lacount, the 13th; Frederick T. Moses, the 18th; and John L. Wilds, the 27th.

It has been erroneously stated that the N.F.P.A. is merely a tool of the insurance companies. True, the insurance companies supply the necessary technical information—where else would you find it? But, after all, they constitute only 20% of the total membership.

The Association has been unusually fortunate in its choice of General Managers: Franklin H. Wentworth from 1909 to 1939, a much beloved crusader of the "fire eater" type, and Percy Bugbee, General Manager since Wentworth's retirement in 1939. Bugbee is able, aggressive and politically astute. Under his direction, the membership, now international in scope, has grown from 4,669 to over 15,000. What is more important, under his guidance the friction seemingly unavoidable in groups drawn from conflicting interests has almost entirely disappeared.

An historical account would be incomplete without at least a passing reference to the efforts that have been made to compete with our system.

The Factory Insurance Association, universally known as the F.I.A., is a "mutual" association of the principal stock fire insurance companies. It was organized in 1890 and has had a somewhat checkered career. Before arriving at its present form it was several times on the verge of disbanding because of bad losses which historically seem to have sprung from internal competition and consequent neglect of fire protection. Its sole avowed purpose was and still is to compete with the Factory Mutual Companies.

The F.I.A. is an underwriting agency with headquarters in Hartford, with limited binding powers for the companies it represents. The first unit was formed in the East; others were formed later in the Middle West and on the Pacific Coast. For many years the F.I.A. and two Midwestern groups, the Western Sprinklered Risk Association and the Underwriters Service Association, all competed not only with the Factory Mutuals but with each other. All this was done under the guise of securing special rates to beat the Factory Mutuals, which, if they had been seeking all the business attributed to them, would have had to maintain a salesman on every street corner.

At the height of this competition the mere mention of the Factory Mutuals to a rating bureau would cause a discriminatory drop in rates. One of our sports of the period was to provide some good friend with the characteristic pink-sheeted Factory Mutual report and let him wave it in front of his agent. It was amazing what that would do to the insurance rate!

In 1941 the Eastern F.I.A. elected as President the late Curtis W. Pierce. Pierce had received his early insurance training as an inspector in the Factory Mutuals, whereafter he rose rapidly in the insurance world and became Vice President of the Continental Insurance Company. He was an able and competent executive, the ablest that the F.I.A. ever had. He combined the different groups across the country into one coherent national organization. By reason of his early Factory Mutual experience he had the knowledge and background necessary to induce his group to try to produce a plausible substitute for our methods.

Of necessity, the F.I.A. is a defensive organization, since the main business of the commercial insurance companies is to write general fire insurance at profitable, non-competitive rates; the Association is maintained mostly for the convenience of agents and brokers who feel that the loss of the fire insurance on the biggest and best-equipped factories would tend to encourage the casualty business to go to the casualty mutuals. Since the average insurance agent does not have the necessary educational background to fit him to furnish the same service to industry as does the Factory Mutual representative, who is a trained engineer, the F.I.A. is, in part, an effort to fill this gap. There is always the psychological handicap that no such expensive organization would be needed if the Factory Mutuals did not exist. There is a similar handicap in the circumstance that the Factory Mutuals' basic principles involve adequate fire protection with resulting low losses and low rates, whereas the F.I.A. is, in effect, a loss leader for the stock companies.

The things that thrive in America are based on competition. Even in a service industry competition stimulates improvement and is of benefit to the buying public. We welcome normal competitive risks if for no other reason than to serve as a yardstick.

● ● ●

There has always been a very limited domestic market for reinsurance, since the majority of stock companies will not reinsure mutuals; consequently we have had to depend principally on Lloyd's and some other foreign companies. But as World War II began to loom up, with its grave threat to our foreign market, the principal mutual companies of the country moved to establish their own reinsurance organization. As a result the American Mutual Reinsurance Company was incorporated in Illinois on June 20, 1941. The Company is engaged in all forms of reinsurance and has operated quite successfully through the years. Carl A. Moses, at that time Executive Vice President of the Firemen's, was a Factory Mutual member of the committee which organized the new company.

When World War II hit the nation, it brought its problems of personnel, of finance, of the implementation by the insurance companies of War Risk insurance. The entire engineering staff of the Factory Mutual Companies concentrated their efforts so successfully on the prevention of fire in key defense plants that there was no important interruption of production in any industry under our supervision.

• • •

In 1951, after forty years of service with the Company, Frederick T. Moses retired in favor of his brother, Carl A. Moses.

During Frederick T. Moses' years of leadership the Company had acquired the control of three companies—Baltimore, Mercantile and Narragansett; branch offices had been established in industrial centers; a market had been created for insurance not eligible for Factory Mutual coverage; excess loss protection had been procured in London Lloyd's. The Company's gross business had increased from some $824,000,000 to over $8,000,000,000. Of even greater importance, he created an organization of alert and aggressive young men and women whose ability has given the Firemen's a national reputation in the insurance world.

Carl A. Moses was born in Ayer, Massachusetts, November 29, 1895. He attended the public schools in Ayer and Moses Brown School in Providence, Rhode Island. He was a student at the United States Naval Academy at Annapolis in 1914 and 1915. He trained as a fighter pilot in the U. S. Army Air Corps in 1917 and 1918 and was injured in an air collision seriously enough to incapacitate him for further service.

Following his recovery he joined the Firemen's as an engineer in Providence and became manager of the New York office when it was opened in 1921. He returned to Providence in 1928 to become Executive Vice President of the Company and was elected President in 1951.

During the three years that he has been President, the volume of business of the Company has increased from something over $8 billion to over $11 billion, the most phenomenal growth in its history!

CARL ALAN MOSES
*President of the Firemen's since 1951.*

"The Burning of the Gaspee" is depicted in this mural, painted by Will S. Taylor for the Firemen's new building.

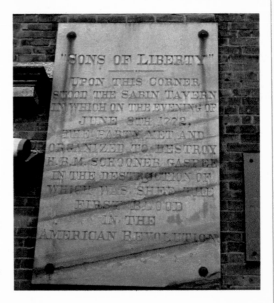

A plaque commemorates the site of the Providence tavern where the deed was planned.

# 6

# Building on Historic Ground

OUR TREMENDOUS GROWTH of business with consequent increase in personnel led us to the conclusion that the needs of the future could best be met by the erection of our own building on a piece of land at 150 South Main Street that we had acquired in 1946.

This location is known locally as Infantry Hall and is in a section so closely identified with the early history of our community that a brief story thereof is of interest.

In 1631 there landed in Boston an English clergyman named Roger Williams. Williams soon found himself in the same position as many others who venture to think differently from their associates. History repeats itself; the Puritans who left England to escape persecution found that they themselves could do a pretty good job of persecuting. Soon the Massachusetts Bay Colony got too hot for Williams; in 1636 he left and founded Providence, where he was soon to be joined by many others.

In 1637 the settlers acquired from the Narragansett Indians a narrow strip of land extending about a mile along the head of the harbor, termed the Great Salt River. The street along the waterfront, in part now our

South Main Street, was known as Towne Street. The settlers lived under extremely primitive conditions, industry was exclusively agricultural. As time went on their crude structures were replaced by small story-and-a-half wooden houses. Even these were to disappear one spring night in 1676 when all but one were burned by the Indians in King Philip's War. When more elaborate houses replaced the old settlement, the area became the residential section for more affluent members of the community.

For perhaps fifty years there was a very slow development of the maritime industry; a few coasters plied back and forth to Newport and there was some commerce with the West Indies.

Prosperity really arrived with the development of privateering, a form of legalized piracy which, because of almost perpetual foreign wars, flourished for nearly three quarters of a century and established the foundation of many a Rhode Island fortune.

The feeling about wars depends upon which side you are on. Certainly the termination of all of these conflicts in 1763 was a source of sorrow to many Colonials. However, the shipowner proceeded to assuage his sorrow by turning to smuggling. Your historian, who is a yachtsman, could never understand why the British revenue cutters should have had difficulty in closing the narrow entrances to Narragansett Bay, but they did, and many a rich cargo from the West Indies landed in Providence.

The historical highlight of this period, at least so far as we in Providence are concerned, is the episode of the British revenue schooner Gaspee. Leaving Newport to pursue a packet headed for Providence, the British captain was tricked into grounding his schooner on what we now know as Gaspee Point.

The Colonials decided to destroy the Gaspee, whereupon a group collected in Sabin's Tavern, then located just south of the site of our new building. The party embarked at night and proceeded with muffled oars to the grounded Gaspee, which they captured and burned about daylight.

In the lobby of our new building there is a mural, "The Burning of the Gaspee," beautifully executed by Professor Will S. Taylor, formerly the head of the Art Department of Brown University.

By the time of the American Revolution, Providence had become a colony dependent upon maritime commerce and the Revolution brought a serious check to the prosperity of the state. Much of this was recovered after the war and in 1790 a statement was made in Congress that there was a greater number of vessels hailing from Providence than New York.

Fires were frequent in the somewhat crude construction of early America and in 1801 part of Towne Street was burned out again, to be once more replaced by a more substantial type of residential construction.

At one time Towne Street was renamed Water Street and, finally, in 1823 part of it was given its present name of South Main Street. Foreign commerce had begun to diminish, much of it to be replaced by the maritime coastal trade. The day of sail was to come to an end, to be replaced by steamers with rail connections to other communities.

As time went on South Main Street started to deteriorate, business was moving to the west side of the river, and when the horse cars appeared on the street, the old families moved away. By the 1890's the area included a collection of flophouses and bars; the old residences housed a motley collection of tenants.

Sometime in the early history of South Main Street, our present site contained "three old wooden buildings described as occupied by a nondescript corps of tenants, keeping hucksteries and grog shops. From the aspect of the buildings and the looks and habits of the tenants and patrons of the shops, it had obtained the name of 'Rotten Row' and was a nuisance to those who lived in the vicinity. The name of one of the tenants of the Row was Prout and, among other things, he kept a bear. It is reported that, when any allusion to them was made, they were referred to in the words 'rascally Prout and his rascally bear.' "*

Fires are the reason for insurance companies. A specific fire we believe to be responsible for the name of our Firemen's Company. In 1754 the inhabitants petitioned for power to purchase a "large water engine" to be paid for by an assessment against the property in that part of Providence considered liable to be destroyed. It was also required that each family be

---

* From a book published by the Rhode Island Historical Society.

provided with two fire buckets, kept filled with water. Fire companies were purely voluntary; there was great rivalry which frequently resulted in riot and bloodshed. On October 10, 1853, a serious fire occurred in a building on North Main Street. Following an established custom, liquor had been distributed to the firemen by bars in that vicinity and, as usually happened, a quarrel occurred between rival fire companies, ending in the murder of a teamster. Under the laws which then existed, police could not interfere with firemen at a fire except by order of the Chief Engineer. Public outcry resulted in the discontinuance of the volunteer system and early in 1854 the first paid fire department was organized. About two months later our company received its charter, taking its name "Firemen's" from the new system.

To return to South Main Street and the story of our new building site, it appears that in 1818 a group of young men, members of a Providence debating society, suddenly decided to form a military organization and in May, 1818, incorporated as the First Light Infantry Company. What debating had to do with it we do not know, but the founders of the Infantry were men of serious thought and purpose; one clause in their by-laws states that they were associated "not for the purpose of parading and ostentation but to form a corps at all times prepared to resist sudden invasion and repel internal commotion."

As was then the fashion, the First Light Infantry did a lot of parading and escorting, but it also served during various uprisings and in the Civil and Spanish American Wars.

On May 12, 1879, the cornerstone of a new building was laid and the building known as Infantry Hall was completed in January, 1880; it was officially opened with a grand military affair which ran for twelve nights. The building was the scene of many brilliant social events, but it was found to be commercially unpractical, and the Infantry lost control; thereafter it was used for many years for miscellaneous entertainment purposes. It was destroyed by fire in 1942.

Following our purchase of the property plans were prepared by Cram & Ferguson, of Boston, architects specializing in office buildings.

After several years' delay, aggravated by the embargo on materials occasioned by the Korean War, plans were completed and construction started in September, 1952, by the Gilbane Building Company of Providence.

The building is Colonial in design, contains approximately 65,000 square feet of floor space, completely sound-proofed and air-conditioned. The space will accommodate a 60% increase in personnel, and there is room in the rear for an addition equal to another 50%.

The pendulum swings and with the plans that the City has for a new highway and the development of this area, South Main Street will in time lose most of its ancient structures and regain much of its former prestige.

It is especially interesting to us that this building was completed and occupied just in time for our Centennial, May 6, 1954.

*The Firemen's new home is built in the Colonial style of old Providence.*

*The weathervane on the tower of the new Firemen's building is a model of the author's schooner* Segochet.

# 7

# Into Our Second Century

---

ON THIS, OUR 100TH ANNIVERSARY, we bring to you the story of our past and of our valued traditions, for we believe they may provide a demonstration of those proven principles of operation that can serve as a guide to the future.

Many words have been written about the details of policy contracts, engineering, loss adjustments. They appear in every annual statement of every Factory Mutual Company; there is no point in repeating them.

The original Firemen's policy insured only against fire, excluding fire loss resulting from invasion, riot and civil commotion. As time went on new processes and new hazards appeared and policy contracts were changed to afford the assured supplementary protection. No one company or individual was responsible for these changes; they represent the fulfillment of the collective wishes of all the policyholders of all the Factory Mutual Companies and they have been provided as the necessity has arisen. Our contracts today protect the property owner against all anticipated property damage, loss of earnings, fixed expenses, and other contingent calamities to the extent permitted by law.

No insurance can more than temporarily compensate a business for the loss of its customers, the loss of jobs, the disruption of its suppliers and the whims of a fickle public diverted to other sources. That is why, although we operate as an insurance company, we think primarily in terms of fire prevention for our clients. Our field men and executives are graduate engineers; so are the staff members of the Engineering Division which we maintain in collaboration with the other Factory Mutual Companies.

We in the Firemen's have devoted much of our effort not to developing a large number of small accounts but to becoming the leaders within the Factory Mutual group in the establishment of a personal relationship with the larger corporations. We have 45 accounts that exceed $50,000,-000 in the value of insurance, eighteen that exceed $100,000,000, ten that exceed $200,000,000, eight that exceed $300,000,000.

These organizations maintain their own insurance departments; they desire association with men who understand their fire protection problems, in other words with men who have the "know how." Their sense of values is such that an insurance connection is not established solely on the basis of price. Public confidence is not always readily measured but it is a key factor, absolutely vital to the success of any business.

These are corporations which frequently own their own mines, forests, oil wells and other raw materials. Through us, they own their own insurance company.

When you read about an institution you are reading about men, since any company is most importantly a collection of people—people grouped together for a common purpose.

As the years go by a company such as ours develops a personality of its own, a personality which in turn influences the attitude of the people within it. Their loyalty and cooperation have made our success possible; words are not adequate to properly pay tribute to them. As we, the Firemen's organization, are composed of individuals selected and trained by the leaders of the past, so in turn will the future reflect our ability in those we have chosen to follow us.

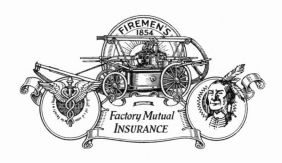

Firemen's Mutual Insurance Company was incorporated May 6, 1854 by William Viall, John Eddy and others not named.

The first officers were John F. Phillips, President, and John Eddy, Secretary and Treasurer.

## PRESIDENTS AND THEIR TERMS OF OFFICE
### 1854-1954

| | |
|---|---|
| JOHN F. PHILLIPS | July, 1854 to November, 1863 |
| ALBERT WATERMAN | May, 1864 to June, 1869 |
| WILLIAM VIALL | March, 1870 to January, 1880 |
| EDWIN BARROWS | January, 1880 to July, 1908 |
| ROBERT W. TAFT | July, 1908 to February, 1909 |
| FREDERICK W. MOSES | February, 1909 to February, 1926 |
| FREDERICK T. MOSES | February, 1926 to February, 1951 |
| CARL A. MOSES | February, 1951 |

# DIRECTORS OF THE COMPANY AND THEIR YEARS OF SERVICE

## 1854-1954

| | | | | |
|---|---|---|---|---|
| ALLEN, CHARLES L. | 1913-1919 | | *FRIEZE, LYMAN B. | 1854-1874 |
| AMES, JOHN O. | 1912-1929 | | *GARDNER, HENRY W. | 1854-1857 |
| ATWOOD, J. ARTHUR | 1912-1949 | | GODDARD, MOSES B. I. | 1874-1875 |
| BANKS, W. N. | 1942-1947 | | GRINNELL, RUSSELL | 1905-1948 |
| BARROWS, EDWIN | 1880-1908 | | | |
| BUCKLIN, E. C. | 1924-1934 | | HARRIS, DAVID S. | 1862-1895 |
| BUCKLIN, HARRIS H. | 1932- | | HARRIS, STEPHEN, JR. | 1855-1895 |
| BURGESS, JOHN D. | 1854-1854 | | *HAWES, ARNOLD C. | 1854-1857 |
| *BURR, EDWARD | 1854-1855 | | HILL, THOMAS J. | 1854-1895 |
| | | | *HOLMES, GEORGE B. | 1854-1879 |
| *CARR, DAVID S. | 1854-1890 | | HUNTOON, HARRISON B. | 1932-1934 |
| CHACE, HARVEY | 1861-1883 | | HUNTOON, MAXWELL C. | 1945- |
| CHACE, JAMES H. | 1877-1913 | | | |
| CHAPIN, WILLIAM P. | 1926-1936 | | JENKS, ROBERT R. | 1929-1946 |
| CUSHMAN, HERBERT E. | 1910-1924 | | JETT, SHELBY M. | 1929-1944 |
| *DAILEY, ALBERT N. | 1854-1877 | | KELLEY, A. LIVINGSTON | 1934- |
| DANIELSON, JOHN W. | 1879-1912 | | *KNIGHT, BENJAMIN B. | 1854-1857 |
| DRAKE, ARCHIE A. | 1947- | | KNIGHT, C. PRESCOTT | 1892-1920 |
| *EDDY, NATHANIEL A. | 1854-1857 | | LEESON, ROBERT | 1947- |
| ELTON, JOHN P. | 1910-1913 | | LIPPINCOTT, CHARLES W. | 1895-1924 |
| EVANS, FRED B. | 1882-1897 | | LIPPINCOTT, HENRY | 1862-1892 |

MAKEPEACE, CHARLES R... 1920-1926

MATTESON, GEORGE W. R.. 1877-1893

MATTHES, MAX H........ 1934-

MAYNARD, FRANK H...... 1897-1918

MEANS, WILLIAM ....... 1918-1929

METCALF, G. PIERCE..... 1942-

METCALF, JESSE........ 1870-1900

METCALF, STEPHEN ..... 1898-1942

MOSES, CARL A......... 1929-

MOSES, FREDERICK T..... 1924-

MOSES, FREDERICK W..... 1909-1928

MOSES, HARLAN T. ...... 1951-

OMWAKE, JOHN ....... 1925-1938

OWEN, CHARLES D....... 1919-1937

OWEN, CHARLES D., JR. ... 1937-1947

PIERCE, THOMAS L....... 1937-1945

*POTTER, NATHANIEL F..... 1854-1854

RICHMOND, FRANK E...... 1913-1942

ROCKWELL, CHARLES B.... 1942-

RUMPF, ARTHUR G...... $\begin{cases} 1927\text{-}1932 \\ 1945\text{-} \end{cases}$

*SAYLES, WELCOME B...... 1854-1861

*SISSON, DAVID .......... 1854-1862

SLATER, HORATIO N...... 1855-1864

SPRAGUE, AMASA ........ 1856-1882

SPRAGUE, WILLIAM, 2ND... 1854-1856

STEAD, THOMAS J........ 1854-1862

STEVENS, FRANK S. ...... 1881-1898

*STONE, PARDON M. ...... 1854-1906

SWIFT, EDWARD W....... 1938-1942

TAFT, ROBERT W........ 1900-1928

TAFT, ROYAL C.......... 1864-1912

*TALLMAN, WILLIAM ...... 1854-1855

THOMPSON, RUPERT C., JR. 1948-

*VIALL, WILLIAM ......... 1854-1880

WATERMAN, ALBERT...... 1860-1870

WATERMAN, JOHN O. ..... 1855-1881

*WHITAKER, ANTHONY B. A. 1854-1860

WILDS, JOHN L.......... 1927-

YOUNG, UDELL C. ........ 1947-

---

* Served on first Board of Directors

99

# BOARD OF DIRECTORS

## JANUARY 1, 1954

HARRIS H. BUCKLIN . . . . . *Vice-President, Interlaken Mills*

ARCHIE A. DRAKE . *Exec. Vice-President, Bibb Manufacturing Company*

MAXWELL C. HUNTOON . *President-Treasurer, Packaging Materials Corp.*

A. LIVINGSTON KELLEY . . *President, Providence Institution for Savings*

ROBERT LEESON . . . . *President, Universal Winding Company*

MAX H. MATTHES . . . *Technical Consultant of the Company*

G. PIERCE METCALF . . . . . *President, Wanskuck Company*

FREDERICK T. MOSES . . . . . . *Chairman of the Board*

CARL A. MOSES . . . . . . *President of the Company*

HARLAN T. MOSES . . . . *Exec. Vice-President of the Company*

CHARLES B. ROCKWELL . *President-Treasurer, The Allendale Company*

ARTHUR G. RUMPF
   *Retired, formerly Secretary-Treasurer, The Studebaker Corporation*

RUPERT C. THOMPSON, JR.
   *Exec. Vice-President, Industrial National Bank of Providence*

JOHN L. WILDS
   *Chairman of the Board, Protection Mutual Insurance Company*

UDELL C. YOUNG . . . *Vice-President, General Foods Corporation*

# OFFICERS

## JANUARY 1, 1954

Frederick T. Moses . . . . . *Chairman of the Board*

Carl A. Moses . . . . . . . . *President*

Harlan T. Moses . . . . . . *Executive Vice-President*

Barton F. Curit . . . . . *Vice-President—Secretary*

Burr F. Gongwer . . . . . . . *Vice-President*

Harry C. Wolf, Jr. . . . . . . *Vice-President*

Max H. Mattes, Jr. . . . . . . *Vice-President*

John W. Shelhart . . . . . . *Vice-President*

David W. Patterson . . . . . *Treasurer-Controller*

Jean M. Legris . . . . *Assistant Secretary—Assistant Treasurer*

Donald H. Robertson . . . . . *Assistant Treasurer*

Frederick C. Morris . . . . . *Assistant Secretary*

H. Bruce Leslie . . . . . . *Assistant Secretary*

Frederick Moses, III . . . . . *Assistant Secretary*

Howard M. Arnold . . . . . . . *Cashier*

# HOME OFFICE STAFF

## JANUARY 1, 1954

150 SOUTH MAIN STREET
PROVIDENCE 1, RHODE ISLAND

### UNDERWRITING DEPARTMENT
F. C. MORRIS, *Assistant Secretary*
H. B. LESLIE, *Assistant Secretary*
F. MOSES, III, *Assistant Secretary*

| | |
|---|---|
| K. S. JOHNSON | H. M. MACOMB |
| W. N. PERRY | H. L. NORCROSS |
| R. E. VIVIAN | S. E. SIMMONS, JR. |

### ACCOUNTING DEPARTMENT
D. W. PATTERSON, *Treasurer-Controller*
D. H. ROBERTSON, *Assistant Treasurer*
E. D. SHELLEY, *Auditor*
H. M. ARNOLD, *Cashier and Purchasing Agent*

### ENGINEERING DEPARTMENT
J. M. HANLEY, *Chief Engineer*
J. O. HERBSTER, *Asst. Chief Engineer*
DOROTHY DOWNS, *Asst. to Chief Engineer*
T. F. HEFNER, *Engineer*

### PERSONNEL DEPARTMENT
JOHN P. CADY, *Executive Assistant*

---

### INSPECTION AND ADJUSTMENT HEADQUARTERS
FACTORY MUTUAL ENGINEERING DIVISION
184 HIGH STREET, BOSTON 10, MASS.
G. F. WAHL, *General Manager*

# BRANCH OFFICES

## JANUARY 1, 1954

MANAGER OF FIELD OPERATIONS
Burr F. Gongwer, *Vice-President*
2140 GRAYBAR BUILDING, NEW YORK 17, N. Y.

## NEW YORK

2140 GRAYBAR BUILDING
420 LEXINGTON AVENUE
NEW YORK 17, N. Y.
J. W. SHELHART,
*Vice-President and Manager*
E. P. HEMPSTEAD, *Engineer*
H. H. GOFF, *Engineer*
C. H. SPRINGER, *Engineer*
G. R. LEHMULLER, *Engineer*
H. N. G. HULTGREN,
*Technical Assistant*

## OHIO

1062 UNION COMMERCE BLDG.
CLEVELAND 14, OHIO
M. H. MATTHES, JR.,
*Vice-President and Manager*
G. M. HALE, *Engineer*
V. J. McWHERTER, *Engineer*
G. C. FARNUM, *Engineer*

## ILLINOIS

1630 CONTINENTAL ILLINOIS BANK BLDG.
231 SOUTH LA SALLE STREET
CHICAGO 4, ILLINOIS
DON CARLEY, *Resident Manager*

## MICHIGAN

1566 NATIONAL BANK BUILDING
DETROIT 26, MICH.
W. C. STYERWALT, *Resident Manager*

## NORTH CAROLINA

1009 JOHNSTON BUILDING
CHARLOTTE 2, N. C.
H. C. WOLF, JR.,
*Vice-President and Manager*
W. J. L. McNEARY, *Engineer*
J. L. PICKLER, *Engineer*

## GEORGIA

1224 CANDLER BUILDING
127 PEACHTREE ST., N. E.
ATLANTA 3, GEORGIA
G. C. WOLF, *Resident Manager*

## TEXAS

BERMAC BUILDING
4101 SAN JACINTO
HOUSTON 4, TEXAS
D. C. FERGUSON, *Resident Manager*

## CALIFORNIA

1022 VAN NUYS BUILDING
210 WEST 7TH STREET
LOS ANGELES, CALIF.
B. M. SHERWIN, *Resident Manager*

# TREASURER'S REPORT

## DECEMBER 31, 1953

## ASSETS

| | |
|---|---:|
| Government bonds | $25,819,625.87 |
| Railroad bonds | 1,133,672.68 |
| Public Utility bonds | 670,318.96 |
| Industrial and Miscellaneous bonds | 36,000.00 |
| Railroad stocks | 601,200.00 |
| Bank and Insurance Company stocks | 2,029,340.00 |
| Public Utility stocks | 6,554,505.00 |
| Industrial and Miscellaneous stocks | 1,822,103.00 |
| Real estate | 1,817,800.32 |
| Premiums in course of collection | 4,344,418.11 |
| Interest accrued | 135,403.32 |
| Loss Fund account | 123,577.00 |
| Cash on hand and in banks | 1,986,609.34 |
| Premium on Canadian Currency balances | 45,048.03 |
| | $47,119,621.63 |

## LIABILITIES AND SURPLUS

| | |
|---|---:|
| Reserve for unearned premiums | $21,966,419.00 |
| Federal Income Taxes due and accrued | 285,000.00 |
| All other Taxes due and accrued | 205,000.00 |
| Losses in process of adjustment | 1,920,554.61 |
| Balances due under reinsurance treaties | 3,186,503.65 |
| Other liabilities | 499,585.06 |
| Total Liabilities | $28,063,062.32 |
| Policyholders' surplus including $500,000 Guaranty Fund | 19,056,559.31 |
| | $47,119,621.63 |

Note: Securities carried in above statement at $1,242,781.46 are deposited as required by law, and such deposits are held for the benefit of all policyholders wherever located. Policyholders' surplus with securities valued at actual market rates would be $18,736,776.44.

# ASSOCIATED FACTORY MUTUAL
# FIRE INSURANCE COMPANIES

|  | Incorporated |
|---|---|
| FIREMEN'S MUTUAL INSURANCE CO. | 1854 |
| ARKWRIGHT MUTUAL FIRE INSURANCE CO. | 1860 |
| BLACKSTONE MUTUAL INSURANCE CO. | 1868 |
| BOSTON MANUFACTURERS MUTUAL FIRE INSURANCE CO. | 1850 |
| INDUSTRIAL MUTUAL INSURANCE CO. | 1875 |
| MANUFACTURERS MUTUAL FIRE INSURANCE CO. | 1835 |
| PHILADELPHIA MANUFACTURERS MUTUAL INSURANCE CO. | 1880 |
| PROTECTION MUTUAL INSURANCE CO. | 1887 |

# COMBINED STATEMENT

## DECEMBER 31, 1953

**COMBINED RESOURCES***

| | |
|---|---:|
| Net Assets at Market Value .............................. | $  256,001,190 |
| Premium Deposits in Force ............................. | 243,941,524 |
| Amount at Risk .................................... | 52,429,687,637 |
| Surplus in Excess of Legal Requirements ................. | 128,552,721 |
| Net Losses ......................................... | 16,659,054 |
| Losses per Million Dollars of Insurance ................... | 318 |
| Assets per Dollar of Loss ............................... | 15 |

| COMBINED LOSSES FOR THE YEAR* | Number of Losses | | Amount of Losses |
|---|:---:|:---:|---:|
| Fire and Lightning ........................ | 5207 | $ | 7,618,000 |
| Sprinkler Leakage .......................... | 649 | | 585,000 |
| Windstorm ............................... | 1587 | | 5,160,000 |
| Explosion ................................ | 270 | | 1,376,000 |
| Use and Occupancy ........................ | 931 | | 3,026,000 |
| Riot and Civil Commotion, Self-Propelled Vehicles and Earthquake ................... | 604 | | 162,000 |

* Estimated as of December 31, 1953

# ACKNOWLEDGMENTS

Although the author alone is responsible for the text of this book, he is indebted to many people, far too numerous to list: to those either directly or indirectly connected with our company; to numerous corporations which furnished the information we have used; to the owners of various photographs; to the many friendly people who have guided us to historical material, particularly the Providence Public Library and the Rhode Island Historical Society. Without their help and cooperation this book would not have been possible.

*This book was designed by*
THORNDIKE, JENSEN & PARTON, INC., 10 EAST 40TH STREET, NEW YORK
ART DIRECTION BY EDWARD A. HAMILTON
ORIGINAL DRAWINGS BY DOUGLAS GORSLINE
ENDPAPERS BY HAROLD G. BREUL
PRINTED BY THE BECK ENGRAVING COMPANY, INC., PHILADELPHIA

## Picture Credits

Adler's, Inc.: 65
Boston American—International: 67
Brown Brothers: 15, 36, 39, 78
Culver Service: 12, 18

Ford Motor Company: 49
Long Island Historical Society: 17
National Board of Fire Underwriters: 14
Providence Public Library: 35

# THE END PAPERS

The painting on the end paper at the front of this book shows the Providence waterfront as it looked in the early days of the 19th century. Sailing vessels are docked in the basin, known as the Great Salt River. Above the brick buildings of Towne Street (now South Main Street) rise the steeples of the First Baptist and First Unitarian churches.

The painting on the back end paper shows South Main Street in Providence as it looks today. The new building of the Firemen's Mutual Insurance Company at right carries out the architectural style of this historic street. In the background may be seen the same steeples that appear in the scene on the front end paper.